In The Winds From My Mother's Mouth

Igoe Brown

Published by Igoe Brown, 2024.

IN THE WINDS FROM MY MOTHER'S MOUTH

First edition. August 9, 2024.

Copyright © 2024 Igoe Brown.

ISBN: 979-8227044020

Written by Igoe Brown.

Table of Contents

To all those who have been or are currently being bullied, harassed, assaulted, abused or degraded. May they find the love that is most life-giving to them.

Again

I-I-I-I I....
Cannot speak
Old Friend, you have robbed me of my lips.
I cannot articulate or express myself
At all.
It has slowly been decreasing.
My poetic ability had been improving
But then I cannot write now.
It has been a slow descent but after 2 decades,
I now understand that you collect another payment.
I am in the full bloom of youth.
I have never known youth. I doubt I ever will.
Yet,
My Darkest Friend, we used to have such meaningful
conversations.
I used to be proud of how intelligent I could come across as,
Because I did not have much else.
Now you make me stutter.
Now it's gotten even worse.
Now I have trouble just having these intelligent ideas.

I like to draw,
I like building with Legos.
I was a really good finger picker for the year that I tried learning
the banjo
I'm a kinesthetic learner,
I learn through doing
and actions.
I like to run my fingertips across walls and surfaces while I walk
pass them having my fingernails lightly graze
But never scratch!
just because I want to know what it feels like
And I need something to do with my hands.
I'm what you'd call,
a tactile person.
So when this ball of stress starts pulsing with my heart beat
It grows with intensity every beat
Getting faster
Getting stronger
Getting wider
Until my whole body is pulsing with those same palpitations
I can't think straight
My thoughts are getting interrupted
I can't do them justice
Even though it's terrifying what I'm thinking
I just keep jumping from terrifying thought to terrifying thought
That I'm not really even sure that
I.

Want.
It.
To.
Stop.
Because then I'm left with sifting through these new discoveries.
Tell me, how do you really feel?
All the while I'm trying to run away from this
Flash back
Panic attack
Metaphorically.
Sometimes literally.
My hands started shaking all on their own.
Did I do that?
I didn't mean to.
I'm sorry hands.
I'll be running my thumb across my fingertips and their nails.
I'll be moving my fingers on my palm like the tides.
I'll be soothing the parts of my body that feel the most stress boiling.
My sternum, collarbone, and neck.
And depending on the inciting incident,
we'll get various different flavors of anxiety attacks.
"Hey baby, you're lookin fine,
Won't you tell me your sign?"
Thank you for reminding me
that this world only perceives this body as a white cis woman
But that still protects me from you crossing the street and hitting
on me in a very different way.
Grief.
Erasure.

Anger.
Paranoia,
While I look over my shoulder for the next 8 blocks and catch a
different bus.
My hands were steadied after the first block and a half and then
immobile rendered in loose fists at my side.
"Your win for gay marriage is a threat to my religion!"
There it is!
I finally wrung it outta ya.
Thanks, mom.
Just walking down the street just listening to music, then
BOOM!
An immediate reminder of how many queer people you've hurt
I'm a hand wringer,
A finger bender,
I need to shake it out.
My anxiety,
big
and
small
You can always see in my hands.

It's **stomp stomp stomp**
Deep voice
Loud **voice**
Angry voice
I know we don't have money
I know that you're stressed
I know that my body is a reminder of our waste
I know
I know
I KNOW
You make me anxious
You make me itchy
I need to leave
I need to throw up
You need to stop
Because literally *anything is better than this*
I've reached the point where I view death as having a better cost
than this
I can't do ***anything*** when you're like this
I can't move
Can't breathe
Can't ***eat***
Even though you're doing this at dinner!
I can't exist because everything will throw you farther
You make me miserable
I don't respond well to your anger!
And it incites anger within

But your wife of 30 years sits silently and lets this play out in
front of her four children
Because this is a healthy way to deal with anger
Because ***this* is a normal thing to be angry about**
Because he's not *angry, he's frustrated*

The best memories I have of it happening were in the car.
You'd pick me up for some reason,
we would sit outside for your son to come out of school.
I think we would get there really early
and you would talk
Not in a way befitting a father talking to their child,
but in a way more suitable for a man talking to his wife—
whom existed—
or a therapist—
whom was abandoned after a negligible amount of sessions.
I would sit there,
Hating it
I felt so gross and itchy
And it was just so intimate, the things you were sharing.
You made me feel like it was my fault that you were feeling these
things!
When you were angry it was my fault.
When you were sad it was my fault.
When you lied and said you were "frustrated" as you berated us,
it was my fault.
When you were happy,
it was never my doing,
according to you and Mom,
I, "was a miserable child".
None of this emotional incest is helped by
the most humanizing thing I have ever witnessed from you,

your dick pic, stored on a computer your pubescent child had
access to.
The regular abuse,
The hitting,
The emotional neglect,
The physical neglect,
The abandonment,
I don't fully understand the ramifications of yet
Other than the cptsd
But this I wonder about.
The fawn response,
Trying so hard to make things go away by making people happy,
In the most insignificant interactions
I would tell you you were wrong for yelling at us
and I would get hit for that
But I always just wanted the sessions of you *using me* to end.
I get held hostage by the most asinine things.
Because of you,
because of what you did.
I've been trained not to move,
to appease the speaker,
the toucher,
just to get it over with.
In service work there's always someone an arm's length away
from assaulting you
One way or another
And people have done it!
To me!
I've just waited for it to be over
Because of how well you trained me to take it

I come back to those dark dark moments
and I don't understand your capacity to live with yourself.
Which is, of course, what you spoke about

Regular Us

The seat is vibrating and everything's vaguely uncomfortable and
vaguely smells of urine
But that's the regular cta for you.
It's midday and we're able to get our favorite seats on the brown
line,
The ones in the back of the car that have a little compartment
and face the car behind you,
The city is moving past in partial view and we're partially
viewing.
Partially not.
It's just regular us
In our regular clothes
On our regular schedule,
In our preferably regular seats
Of course, only when I'm capable of not talking, because I
regularly love to talk
And when we talk.
But that's just regular us.
You're sitting on my left closer to the window,
(In the seat with the less leg room—I'm just saying)
And in front of me on the right is the emergency exit to that car
behind us.
I'm really hoping no one decides they need it
Because we're in our regular positions,
You scrunched up over your iPod
And me slouched and spread out with my crossed legs resting on
the wall of the car.

But regular us includes what had become a new regular for me.
In terms of the length of time I've been with this new regular
length of leg hair,
It's been much shorter in my relationship with leg hair
Than the length of time I've been with this regular in my
relationship with you.
So whenever someone walks by and sees these furry legs
I'm definitely not over being self-conscious.
And that's regular me.
But the best part of regular us is that you don't care about my
furry legs.
Regular me is no longer regular because I've had to and I'm
continuing to adapt to having a person to be regular with.
It's now not shit to have a regularity in my regular.
A regular 'us' in which I know the other half of the 'us' doesn't
hate me or think I'm annoying.
I think. For the most part. Probably.
A regular in which the other half doesn't pity me or think I'm
messed up
An other regular half that doesn't give a shit that these are my
regular clothes
And that if they're not perfectly regular,
No worries
The regular to my regular gives me the freedom to be whatever
the fuck kind of regular I want to be,
And I have never in my fucking life had to not conform to be
regular.
My regular is mine and their regular is theirs.
A regular that I can be regular with.
Which is what makes it a regular us.

We'll probably get off at that new stop we've been trying out,
Changing our regular schedule,
And take that regular route when we get off at this new stop
And going to our regular work space
Before our regular class
And continue with this regular life.
It's only when we take that newly regular route that I notice I've never had that.
A regular me in a regular life as a part of a healthy regular us.

Resemblance

I know it's silly
But I really can't help the association.
You were drunk,
You made a promise.
I was excited. I thought we had plans.
Until this morning that is.
You don't often remember your drunken declarations
I do.
I haven't been drunk enough lately and spent enough inebriated
time with you
To forget the next morning.
But last night I was sober.
I hadn't left our room
I hadn't left my bed
You got home at 4 am.
Your proposition was difficult for me to accept.
I felt like you cared for me
That you wanted to spend time with me
But the morning you didn't bring it up
And I couldn't bring myself to ask for your attention
I've learned since I was 4 crying and yelling
with a little voice at my father
He had to cancel on something we were supposed to do together.
I couldn't remember the last time I did anything with either
of my parents outside of our regular routine and without my
brothers.

Now Dad was ditching me for a Weird Al concert with the boys because he got tickets from work.

I wanted to go.

I liked Weird Al.

But it wasn't for little girls.

It was for my brothers.

It was for my cousin.

It was for my Dad and Uncle.

Not for Mom.

(Though she really didn't like Weird Al and someone had to look after me)

He looked guilty.

He sounded sad.

I ran away up the stairs to cry in solitude.

The lies and disregard from my parents was killing me.

But now I know he could never understand the kind of restrictions he placed on his child.

I've come to learn not to expect things from anyone.

It's a symptom of my abandonment issues.

It's why I sat in the living room today

In the chair adjacent to the couch you were in

Silent.

It's why I went back into our room and back into bed after that one episode of Suits ended.

I'm not going to ask anything from you.

I'm sad and I'm broken and I promise to forget the feeling I got

Just as I'm going to forget how you hurt me after Kya's birthday party

Because you were high and you thought it was funny.

I won't tell you.

It's embarrassing and needy.
You said last night what you've often said before
"I hate my feelings. Feelings make you weak"
You were joking.
But I've been feeling so much lately
So it didn't feel like a joke.
And I started listening to The Front Bottoms
While carving up my skin
Thinking about him
Thinking about him
The lights are off now
And there's a flash flood warning
But I like the rumble of thunder and the flash of lightning
Outside our window
And I didn't clean the cuts this time

        (I haven't done so the past few times)

I'm still thinking of him
When you were drunk you said
"Out of the 2 of us, you're the darker one. You've got the most
crap"
I'm sorry you've reminded me of my father.
You wouldn't like my parents.
You've never met them
But I feel it the same.
Deep in my bones

Color Wheel of Anger

I'm mad
I'm mad
I'm mad
I'm so fucking mad
It's red. *Seething* red
It's pulsing in my body pushing through one body part to the
next
Setting the tempo of the fists I'm going to pound into your face
Of the cutting remarks that you will *not* withstand
Blood running down your face and it feels *right*
It's green like your snake. That sonofabitch
The poison in her teeth, transferred to mine
So fast you cannot see, you cannot hear,
The yellow, the green, the *toxic* gas is *all* of me choking *all* of you
Until you lie on the floor twitching in pain, your face turned
green
And I told you I was mad.
You fucking knew it
But you didn't listen
You never fucking listen
I'm screaming from the top of a building, tears streaming down
my face and you are working to forget this!
Knife in my hand, we'll see whose blood is pounding out after
this.
Because you *will* know I'm mad
And I am mad
So *fucking* mad

And you couldn't stop this irate fire if you *tried*

Anger is so much easier to feel

The anger isn't as frequent anymore
well neither are the flashbacks or the terror
now it's just a hollowness in my chest

Heartbreak

That's so much harder to feel
The anger
that's justified, it's righteous, it's motivating
I can make someone feel pain for making me suffer.
That's strength
But this?

I lay about feeling shitty
feeling heavy, empty in my chest
(Someone hurt me)

That's weakness
And what am I supposed to do with that?

I wish I could be angry
I wish I could act on my anger
But now I just feel it when I get fucked over at work
or at cops
It felt so good fantasizing about violence
about publicly yelling at my abusers
about smashing the bottom off an empty wine bottle and
stabbing Brett Kavanaugh with it

Now I have is this low to moderate depression keeping me sedate

People hurt me

I run away from people

The people that have hurt me the most

I live with

So I stay away from people

I miss the people that loved me

That understood me

That matched my compassion for others and helped me make my own self compassion

Tick tick tick: tick tok
The clock is about to strike 20
Tick tick tick
The clock wasn't supposed to have this many hours
Time is so weird
I don't know what time is anymore
But I don't know what my hands are anymore though, so
Shrug
Tick tick tick-tick tick tick tick
Time is turing
I think
Time is going fast
(or slow?)
I don't know what's happening
But it's all passing me by...
And by...
And down by the bay
I still don't know what's going on and I'm thinking of when
where we drunkenly sang that song on

the way to Wolf's place for Halloween trying to take
the brown line but it wasn't running because it was
the middle of the World Series. The streets were filled
with people. It was amazing. I was Rosie the Riveter.
You were Steven Universe. It was only amazing
because I was massively drunk. It was a good memory.

Before Connor got hurt

But nothing's a good memory now
Everything's bad
Bad bad bad bad bad bad bad
All those terrible things I wrote about last week when I was glad
you weren't there
In our room
So I could cry myself to sleep
It was the first time since starting this that I've cried about it
I feel like I'm drunk
Like I'm drunk on....
Speed
Climax

    But constantly
    Everything is peak
    Pith.
    I never was able to rythme it well with Will Smith

And that poem I wrote last week about all the terrible terrible
memories
About all the pain
I've been doing better at keeping them away!
I cried myself to sleep on Wednesday
But I'm just having vague impressions of them
Except now
Now, when I'm pacing on Anmol's floor
You haven't met her yet, but she's great
She's really great
Which is why I don't want to punch her wall
No, I really want to punch her wall

Like, really bad.
Just fuck it, DePaul and fuck you wall
And it would feel so good on my hand
I would punch it till my knuckles were bloody and torn

> With blood dripping down my arm until it dried
> rusty red in my arm hair like my menstrual blood on
> my legs in my dreams or when I get out of the shower
> and I forget that some had drip drip dripped down my
> legs and it dries and I have to bathe my legs later or I'll
> get crusty blood on clean towel.

Blood
Bathe
Baptism in the godforsaken Nile
My knuckles
And that wouldn't be enough
I see myself laughing
I see myself smiling
With bloody hands
I did that
I want that
I turn again for the millionth time while pacing.
No.
You shouldn't
You want to but you shouldn't
You shouldn't violate this space that she has graciously allowed
you to enter into
Particularly today when you were out of the blue
She has a scheduled patient in the waiting room

I try and occupy myself with looking but not touching the things
in her office
She has books
Real and Imagined Fathers, Behavioral Psychology,
She has some henna sketched out on her cork board at her desk
It's for hands. It goes around the wrist. Front and back
I've been meaning to tell her that it's beautiful and well crafted
I will. When she comes back
I'll segway with how Afyia has been doing henna lately

"That henna you have sketched out, it's absolutely
beautiful. My friend, their Pakistani", you don't want
to support culturally appropriative henna, "they've
started doing henna. I've been meaning to tell you
that it's amazing since our first appointment"

I still want to punch her wall
I try and look at myself in her mirror
It strikes me that I'm not really sure how I look

I have these two annoying whiteheads on the inside of
my nose that have been a pain in the butt but I also
haven't really been showering or washing my face so I
get why they're there. Taking care of my body is hard. I
don't have time for that. And what's the point, it's just
gonna get dirty by the end of the day. (*You're another
day older*). But I think I look okay. I'm not concerned
that this image is me. (Who is me?) it's just kinda like,
"Ka-chow! Hey there fella!"

Ha ha. I'm a fella. Fella fella fella.

Turn to look out the window.
Tick tick tick tick tick
I was just pacing in the other room
The younger woman, she had brownish auburn hair. Long and wavy.
(she's in training, Anoml said)
She smiled at me when I said I really wanted to pace.
I don't see what's so funny about it
I told her quite plainly how restless I was and she could see it and I said it might be the drugs
What's funny about that? Why is my reaction to medicine for my mental illness funny? I pace all the fucking time. Now I just feel like I have an adequate excuse
With this I just felt like no one would laugh
I was pacing
Back and forth
Back and forth
Tick tick tick tick tick tick
And I had unwrapped a cherry jolly rancher with my mouth and hand
1 hand, not 2
And I plopped it in
There was still a bit of the cellophane wrapper still on it but I picked it of with my teeth and spat it into the trash can like a pro
But my hands weren't doing enough so I picked up the only literature in the room

A different room, by the way. Not Anoml's room. It was a group therapy room. With wide windows. Lots of light. There were 2 lamps and 3 chairs. 2 comfy chairs and one plain plastic chairs. I wanted to turn on the lights. They wouldn't've done anything really. I just wanted to turn them on

So this thing I was "reading"

It was an emergency pamphlet thing

I glossed over it

I don't remember what it said

I looked at the mental health emergency and I said, "Dat me!"

In some part wondering if any of this was going to happen to me

I was pacing and reading but not retaining

I can't retain right now

And I would look across the parking lot into this balcony

It was beautiful

Anyway, I was really distracted by it so I'm trying to distract myself with it again.

Look at the pretty flowers

Look at the beautiful shade

Is that person still out there?

(Inside jokes with myself)

No, they went inside.

Distract distract distract

What's that thing that's behind Anmol's chair? Aw, there's a framed note from people that she worked with one time. Aw, people love Anmol. I'm glad. I'm a shit. Part of me is interested in the fact that I am very much not a part of that. Apart. And that shit behind her chair are a bunch of shoes.

It's nice to see more of her life. She's got a life. It's weird when you share so much with certain people but then you don't have the type of relationship where they share back
That's kinda like us
Ha! Haha!
That's not funny
Tick tik tik tik tiktitktitk
Pace
Punch the wall
Punch the wall
Punch the wall
Sensation of punching the wall
I bite my hands instead
Part of me wants to draw blood
But the human body can't do that
It's not supposed to be able to do that
I'm not sure if that's true
I know that from suzanne collins
Fuck you, suzanne collins.
I never liked your work
It was from the hunger games.
Catching fire, I think.
The worst one
That woman, the one who bites off a body part of another contestant, I want to be able to do what she does.
I want these fingers *off!*
Tickticktickticktickticktickticktcitkticktickticktickticktickticktick
I stop
Tickticktickticktickticktickticktcitkticktickticktickticktickticktick
In front of the wall

The place I've been thinking about
Tickticktickticktickticktickttcitktickticktickticktickticktickticktick
I know it wouldn't be enough
Ticktickticktickticktickticktcitktickticktickticktickticktickticktick
Hands on the wall
The plaster pricks my skin at least
Ticktickticktickticktickticktcitktickticktickticktickticktickticktick
PUSH
I push the wall
Pressure
More pressure
Break the wall
Ticktickticktickticktickticktcitktickticktickticktickticktickticktick
It creaks
Tok
No
Not to Anmol
I saw myself again
I saw myself laughing
I saw myself not getting enough
I saw myself going and going and going and smiling from ear to
ear
Madman, Psycho, Skitzo
My heart begins beating again but it's painful
It's pushing blood into my veins that doesn't deserve to keep me
alive
Those are things I think
Those are images that others have put into my mind and I have
kept. them. there.
Tok

Hands shaking
They still want to be hurt
Tok
This is why i need to be hospitalized
Crazy!
Freak!
That's not news
Tickticktickticktickticktickticktcitktickticktickticktickticktickticktick
I sit down
Kaleb, I'm so scared.
I hope you're still downstairs
I wrote a poem today about potatoes
I have to sit on my hands. I can't have them touching things
I'm crying

Kiss me, I'm Irish

Potato
Potato
Potato
I
Am
A
Potato
But not like in a self deprecation type way when people tag their
selfies
Like
I'm a potato
It's the word that always comes to me
"Think of a word!" People say
(The situation occasionally arises)
Potato
It's always a goddamn potato
It's the most Irish thing about me

On the public patio
sitting on a bench
sun beating at my back
whispers all around

(Of nature:
The birds,
tweeting distantly and intimately,
Flower leaves and petals stirring
Wind hitting my ears.)

(And of the city:
People chatting
Phones dinging
Shoes and cars and bikes squeaking
The smell of an Indian food truck
Music from someone's car
Shade from the awning
Bark from the bench,

All dimmed and brought to me by the winds
surrounding me,
Engulfing me.
Caressing me.
These winds are not from my mother.
They exist.
I exist.
These winds are not from my mother.)

I smile at the wind in my leg hair while my dress gets swept about.

This is not
a dichotomy
that I fit
into presently.
When you choose
to dehumanize
in exchange
for outdated and
dualistic,
exhaustive in speech,
and also
male supremacist
grammar, we,
societally,
deny historically
and presently
grammatically correct
language as
adequate for our
modern-day
communication.
You uphold
systems that oppress.
But most basically,
you are committing
violence against me.
You do not

See me;
Hear me.

To My Fictional, Future Lover

I've never written a love poem
I've never had experiences so that I could understand them even
"Love" doesn't come up as a suggested word on my phone
It's a word I'm acquainted with
But we don't know each other well
I've got a friend crush on love
But I've never been **in** love
I love things
I love people, too
Fiercely so.
And while I firmly believe that my platonic love for these people
is, for example,

> on par with my parents' deep romantic and sexual love
> for one another,

I still say,
"No, I *really* like you.
Like, more than a friend."
As if this person has been upgraded to romantic interest from a
platonic relationship.
There's nothing to be achieved.
These aren't the same scales.
So I've got abandonment issues and depression and anxiety
Which have a nest deep inside my chest
And come out to play rather often.
(Though I suppose it's not playing in the way you might think.
They play among

themselves fighting for dominance. They play with
me. I do not consent.)

It makes it hard for me to love.
I need a lot of affirmation in return
Which I don't usually get.
I'll look for your faults.
But don't worry!
I'm more interested in mine.
I'll imagine our parting of ways
As long as I'll know you,
Seconds after we meet even.
Even if it's your fault,
Even if you do something wrong,
It will be my fault.
I'll have done something.
At the very least, I'll have deserved it.
At 20, I don't know love and that's not a surprise
In many ways I'm still a child
But that I don't think I'll ever know love,
Or rather the love I need,
Is troubling.
I'm writing to you,
My fictional future lover.
I hope you know love before you know me.
I hope your universe is filled with unimaginable joy.
I hope you know lovely, fulfilled, and whole people.
I hope that you are one of them.
I hope that I will be the first and the last sad and broken person
you love.

I hope you never have to bear that pain again.
I hope, selfishly, that your love and my love for you make me
understand love poems.
I hope I will write some poems about you.
I want to have proof for myself that I have felt love.
To all those whom do,
To all those whom will,
I know loving me is hard
And when I throw around
"I love you"s,
What I really mean to convey is
Thanks, for loving me.
These things,

      (As well as other faults not listed here)

Don't make it easy
But you've made it easy to love you.
So thank you. I love you.
And you, my fictional future lover,
I'll hold onto the belief that you maybe aren't so fictional
If anything, to help me believe that one day we'll know love
together,
Whatever your face may be
And that I deserve to know love
Or at least I will
That one day I'll stumble through love,
Knowing what I'm doing even less than I do now,
That one day I'll have a someone
To wake up next to,

To share all of my pent up physical affections with

    (I've got some pretty creative ideas I think, too.
    Apparently nose kisses are too intimate for friends.)

To know what it is to be loved.
To have the experiences necessary to understand love poems.
To my fictional future lover:
I await your call.

To be perceived and conditioned as a woman and a girl

And then I was caught up in the winds from my mother's mouth
With the reminder of all of my failures
Of what their miscarried child could have provided
Of Jack and was he queer?
I think he was, how can anyone know
HE'S NOT HERE TO SPEAK FOR HIMSELF
Is there any escape from these fates for us?

     Is there?
     Is it true?

The oppression that we face will never go away
And yet I still have so much privilege
And there are so many people of color that I would give all of it
to
But I can't because
I DIDN'T ASK FOR THIS
And I still have so far to go
Why can't I cry?
Why can't I wash faster

     Why
     Why
     Why can't I

I went to bed in my mom pants that night.

I have been haunted by the woman that I was told about since
that night.
I was ready to get up and go to her the second she was
mentioned.
That second.

> I couldn't
> I can't
> Why can't I

I was surrounded by 3 men
With 3 different perspectives
But still
I had to define mansplaining that night
Because I was seeking refuge, avoiding my friend that was guilty
of it
And I didn't go to her
Why didn't I go to her
What happened to her
I'm sorry that I wasn't there for you
I'm sorry that the man who reported it to me couldn't be there
for you either
I'm sorry that men are instead more concerned in being there for
themselves
Such as the one who may have attacked you.
I would have been willing to risk my self preservation for you.
...
Because I dare you to find a woman that has never been assaulted
in one form or another

But then, women are taught to expect assault because our bodies
are not our own
Often times politicized and laws are in place to regulate them
So that might be even easier than I implied.
it's just that, THIS IS MY LIFE
THESE ARE OUR LIVES
And I'm done with your so-called opinion.
*MY opinion matters more than your "objective" thoughts on my
fucking life*
Because your thoughts on my feelings are irrelevant
It doesn't change them

    Why can't I?

I asked it then as I sat immobile with a mug that said "home" and
was empty
I asked it then
I had asked it the entire day
But whY COULDN'T THOSE MEN ASK IT AS WELL?
This is my life
And there is no break,
No separation from the struggle
And I can't sleep when this is real
When it's my truth
My burden
Wha*t happened to her?*

Bloodlust

It's a bloodlust
For **my** blood
I have so many points of stimulus
But there's never enough being catered to
It's like masturbating
Just as shameful
Just as private
The same frenzied state
Moving my body to get the release necessary
Sometimes it's just my body on my body
Other times I need tools to make it better
The same high afterwords
The same peaceful decent
The same clean up period
The same exhaustion, preparing me for sleep
In both I'm always disappointed
I am incapable of serving myself

    My own needs
    I don't actually know orgasm in this area
    (I would never want to do this to anyone else)

All I want is my blood cascading down my arms
Dark and thick and clumpy

    Like my menstrual blood

Warm and easily flowing

Like when I donate it with the tubes heating the outside of my forearm

Wetting and making my hairs stick down

Like my leg hair when I dip it in water

Slow

So I can enjoy it and commit it to memory

I want my body to look as war torn as I am

In The Winds From My Mother's Mouth

I have known this place differently than you have
I have seen this place the dead of night
I have seen the mist that covered the land
I have watched the grass grow and the rain clouds descend
I have seen the sun rise and the day devour the night
I have seen this place when it is dead
and empty
and isolated
and nothing familiar is present
I have mapped these lands
I have known them in a time of loneliness
I'm not like you
I have not known it as an academic school
Or a lasting home
Or a place I truly call my own
I have not known it
In harsh winters with wind and snow
I have known it instead
In bright summer's ungodly hours
And the heavy summer rain
There's a dome above this place
Above this valley
So that the night skies above are starless and bible black.
This place is Catholic
And yet I have not known it to be Catholic

This dome above is keeping in the heat that allows for these
damaging Catholic qualities to live inside these grounds without
its Life Source
So I walk aimlessly here
And there
Allowing the winds to guide me
Above to the hill and down to the site in which we are waiting
for the Messiah
I follow the artificial light for the stars are all out
That night in the eye of the storm
Once safety had fallen
And I had thought I had found security in myself and in my life
I walked up the hill
That I never had before
I craved to see the summit,
I craved to see the campus aglow in the night-light and misted
landscape
I craved to avoid Mary's place of residence.
I craved to find a home with her.
During my pilgrimage I'm sure you pushed me
As the breath of God had pushed the storm
Through your mouth the winds compelled me to climb higher as
the storm came forth once more
You now know me in full
And your wind guided me towards the summit
Towards the mother that you never were
Towards the acceptance that I sought
Towards unconditional love not tolerance
And hope
Yet when I reached the Blessed Mother,

Standing arms stretched,
Your winds forced me into her stone embrace.
At my back you and your God brought the rains forth
Striking my coat and skin at harsh angles.
So as I grasp her hand
I try to read aloud her prayer,
Written in drenched stone,
And I yell into the night
The storm surges around me creating destruction
With winds going every which way and rain hitting my face
Leaving my whole body soaked
But the only thing I felt
Was rejection
I pleaded,
Was it a test?
I tried again
And winds picked up pushing me now away from the statue.
I asked for forgiveness,
I tried,
All I wanted was what you had, what everyone around me at
mass had,
What everyone else at home had.
But what your winds gave me was rejection.
And that is what Catholicism means to me
It is the manifestation and possibly the creator of my feeling of
otherness.
The storm that you have brought to me has redistributed the
heat and confusion that have grown and
Risen within the summer dome of this place as I have known it.
It instead swarms around me now,

As the Madonna rejected my hand
It turns cold and ruthless
It hurts me and pains me to my core
To see you and your God,
To show me the real truth that has been hidden from me
But I have known within the darkest confines of my heart.
The wind is from your mouth
You move me in directions that I have no desire to follow
You push me towards myself
You push me away from myself
You push me into my future and into my past
You push me into the church that your God has now shown me
the truth to
Not that I do not belong, but that I never did.
And you forced my hand
Into that which is not mine, never has been, never will be
Your wind consumes me
They surround me in confusion and fear
They follow me
No matter where I go
They always find a way into my life
But only when and where I do not want them
All the wind does
Is remind me of you.

I tend to tell the story of my birth

    (One that no cis people ever have)

Like this:
I start off with "They all thought I was going to be a boy"
And end with "then I came out instead saying
'What even is gender anyway?'"
But still you had to change everything from boy to girl
From blue to pink
Because God forbid someone mistake your daughter for your
son

    (Unlike all the other times since then)

With the name your chose for me, unfit for a girl
Name pulled out of his ass,
Body pulled out of her cervix.
In these past 20 years on this earth
I have thought for the past 14
That I should die.
And that is not something that you,
My brothers,
Can ever really understand.
Because I was going to die because I wasn't their son.
I saw how they treated their sons.

    (I saw how their sons treated me vs each other.)

(I saw how the world treated us differently.)

They wanted their sons as something more than just an object to
serve.
And I could never be the daughter they wanted.
They forced me into that
Pretty Pink Ballerina Princess costume

(But I wanted it)

Just not as much as I wanted to be my brother's army man or
Captain Kirk.
Because that's what I couldn't have
And army men and astronauts get to do so much more than
Ballerina Princesses.
And they're not completely fictional either
...
I was angry enough that my hands were shaking in fists
And I felt good about that.
I knew I was angry and I felt like I was finally acting like angry
people act
But you mocked me
Which was okay
My hands were silly anyway
Ugly
Shouldn't be looked at
Man hands
As your Jerry Seinfeld had me convinced
But Dad, you were even madder at me for being mad that you
picked me up off the ground in my little backpack with 5th grade
calculator and homework

And you continued yelling
And you shook me about
And I was crying with more anger
But mainly fear
And confusion

    (That's what characterized my inner turmoils for the
    next few years:
      Mainly fear and confusion.)

I wanted to hurt myself.
I wanted to kill myself.
I thought about it a lot.
I read *The Color Purple* 3 times every Christmas from ages 10-13
But I couldn't harm myself
It was against God's will
I would go to Hell
But I was already going to Hell anyway
Because I really liked girls.
I didn't let myself know it.
But I knew it
So I better not risk it
I didn't understand until I read
Of that this too sullied flesh would melt
Or that the everlasting had not fix'd / his Canon 'gainst
self-slaughter
When mom finally let me when I was 12
"You're evil and hell-spawn and dirty and ugly, and you must
suffer through life accordingly"
That's what it said at the pulpit

That's what it said on TV
In the newspapers
Sometimes at school
And, *You. Never. Said. Any.thing. To. Con.tra.dict. It.*
But I didn't understand until I read *Hamlet* at 12
So I don't want you to watch TV because it makes you think of me
Because when I think of you when watching TV it's not good things.
I don't want you to go to places that reminds you of me
Because those were places I left because they made me feel shitty.

Untitled

You're demeaning about my complaints of the activity I don't want to do
I scream and I cry
You complain about my hair type as you push from the top of my head down, through tangles
I scream and I cry
You spank me for being too difficult to brush the hair of
I scream and I cry
You separate me from my brothers, so I don't teach them disobedience
I scream and I cry
You don't give me food because I'm too fat, but I haven't eaten all day
I scream and I cry
You don't let me play with our neighbors because the girls are older and slutty
I scream and I cry
You say something mean and I get angry so you pick me up and try to shake it out of me
I scream and I cry
That fight made me late to school
I sit and I cry
You push me towards people that like to hurt me
I sit and I cry
You don't help me when my one friend leaves me
I sit and I cry

When I tell you that I'm always sad and want to die you tell me all the great artists have struggles
I sit and I cry
I'm finally going to leave you and you instill the fear of independence in me
I sit and I cry
3,000 miles away you force me to explain in detail a sexual assault that happened a decade ago as payment if I want to come home
You dismiss it
You hang up
I lay down
I can't cry

About the Author

Brown currently lives in Pennsylvania writing away their anxieties in a politically and literally turbulent climate.

www.ingramcontent.com/pod-product-compliance
Lightning Source LLC
Chambersburg PA
CBHW051459140726
47987CB00006B/2781